20,000 Words In 4 Days –

Write Faster, Outline Better And Write More Every Day!

Written by Zak Khan

Copyright © Zak Khan

Disclaimer:

in any form of binding or cover other than that in which it is published without a similar condition including this condition, being imposed on the subsequent purchaser.

Table Of Content

Using The Outer World To Create Your Inner World

The End Is Night

Introduction

I'm no stranger to the torment of writing. Yes, for some, writing is a pleasure. At time it's truly enjoyable for me too and I consider myself a full time writer but being able to churn out page after page without any immediate rewards takes a toll on any writer.

Failure, on the other hand, leaves a sour taste in your mouth and it's twice as horrible for a writer. All we have is our work. And when your work fails to pay the bills and meet your expectations, failure looms over your head like a dark cloud.

It turns something pleasurable into a daunting task.

As an indie author, I believe there are two paths. The first path is a journey that depends largely on luck, originality, marketing skills and commitment. This is the path some would call - Zero to Hero. A few lucky individuals celebrate bestselling success upon their entrance.

The second path, one which I find myself on, depends largely on persistence, mass production and pure resilience. It's being able to write without fail even when you constantly fail. No single book may ever become a bestseller but having such a large amount of average performing books build you into an established author.

With that being said, by reading this book you will learn:

- How I write 5000 words a day without fail.

- Practical techniques to get started on an idea.

- An array of ideas I use to craft a book quickly.

- The three stages of a plot.

- Easy to use principles to level up your word count.

- How to never face writer's block.

- 5 Essential writing tips

- The 3 arc formula

- And more...

It is said that the average reader only absorbs 11% of information from a single read. With that statistic in mind, I strongly urge you to read this book 5 - 10 times to drastically improve the amount of content you absorb in a manner that promotes learning.

Last but not least, read with the intention of learning.

Whether you're a newbie or an expert, whether you already know the information I'm about to share with you or not, read with the intention of learning. Put aside any fear, reservations and arrogance before reading and adopt the mindset of a hungry learner.

Let's get started...

The First Sentence

It's hard, isn't it?

I know.

Trying to find the right words to begin is often one of the hardest things to do. Regardless of how much plot you've planned, penning that very first sentence is so difficult it leaves you battered and depraved.

Maybe I'm being a bit melodramatic but I've learnt how not to be stuck on the first sentence. The trick is to not think about you as the writer.

Instead, focus on the reader. What could you say, in the sharpest, fastest and potent form possible to get a reader hooked?

Give that some thought and use it every single time you start a new book or chapter.

If you noticed, I began this chapter stating something that YOU have a problem with. I already know that most writers battle with writing the first sentence - that's why I named the heading of this section after it.

But I took it a step further and thought about **why it's hard, how**

does it feel and **what are the solutions**. And of the three, the question that has an answer with the strongest impact is the one that most writers resonate with.

Writing the first sentence **is HARD.**

The fact that it's hard and difficult means you most likely have many unwanted hate and anger towards that problem. So, in turn, I used your frustration and problem as a way to establish a connection between you and me.

Makes sense?

Let's talk about this more.

A first sentence should be impactful and captivating. Once upon a time may not cut it anymore. But then again, it's one of the most well-known storytelling phrases so I see no reason why you couldn't start with that. In fact, most writers avoid using once upon a time as a starter which makes it all the more useful to you. Heck, I've even used it in my description.

The idea of writing is to accomplish one intricate thing - **transfer an idea from your mind into the reader's mind.**

In other words, make him think what you want him to think. To do that, you have to write in a manner that achieves that target in the quickest and most effective way possible.

Writing and reading are not isolated actions. In fact, they are interrelated. Meaning, if you don't enjoy writing something, the reader is not going to enjoy reading it.

That's a rule I live by.

To up my word count and write more, I only focus on writing things that I enjoy writing. And then I read it as a reader. Difficult to do but I try and if I don't enjoy reading it for some reason, I often know exactly why and how to edit my writing to make it enjoyable.

So, reading and writing are interrelated. By doing both, you improve your work and the time you spend working.

As a rule of thumb, read only after you finish a chapter or a book. It's very easy to get distracted and lose focus when writing so I encourage you to do this in a step by step manner.

Write -enjoy- **read** - enjoy or **edit** and **enjoy.**

Once you master the art of writing to completion, then you can stop and go as much as you want. And that brings me to the reasons why you have such a hard time writing the first sentence.

1. Lack Of Practice. It's simple math that addition grows a number.

1 + 1 = 2. Keep adding one to that equation and you can go on forever.

No driver is born with the skillset to drive a manual car. I guarantee you, 99% of people on this planet will not be able to master manual driving the first time they try.

Some things in life can only be achieved through practice.

And I believe writing the first sentence may just be one of those things. The more you practice, the better you become.

To make this easy on you, I have an activity for you to do once every day. At the beginning of your writing session, I want you to write 5 lines describing or explaining the plot of your favorite movie.

You can stop after the first paragraph but do this every day.

Use this small activity to build experience.

I give you a few days to 2 weeks and you'll never struggle to write the first sentence ever again from a technical standpoint.

It may not be the most gripping first sentence and you may not be happy with it but you'll never quit before you start ever again. Once you scale this initial hurdle, the rest is much easier and a lot more enjoyable.

2. Placing Too Much Emphasis On The First Sentence. I've studied marketing for the last 2 years and I'm not much of a fan but it was essential to learn everything I could since most of my freelance clients were in the inbound marketing sector.

I scoured the internet, almost daily, searching for fundamental principles that guarantee good marketing and copy.

I learnt the following - *The first sentence is your hook.*

Meaning that it determines whether or not someone will read on. It has to be the best sentence you write.

I find this to be inaccurate and untrue.

What many people fail to realize is that the first sentence of a book is not the first thing they read. I dare you to open up a book right now and show me on which page do you find the first sentence of the story.

I guarantee you it won't be on the first page. Often, there's an acknowledgement and forward that fills the first few pages. But, even before those, what's the very first thing people read.

The Title or *The Headline.*

That's right.

The very first words people see are your hook - not the first sentence. When a fish bites bait, it automatically bites the hook. Turn your reel and you'll pull the fish closer to the surface of the water and before long, into your hands.

The very same could be said about writing and reading.

A book's cover, title and catch line are the three things a reader first notices and reads. If they're intrigued and open the book, they've taken your bait. The hardest part is already done. All you have to do is start turning the reel by simply furthering the curiosity with the next best line that compliments your title or headline.

I'm going to use 2 examples below.

Headline #1 - **This 23 Year Old Kid Lost 47 Pounds in 4 Weeks**

First Sentence - *"Mark, once a skinny-fat kid with chubby cheeks, now a Greek god with abs of steel..."*

Book Title #1 - **Night Crawlers**

First Sentence - *"They're everywhere. These little crusty bastards are now skin deep. I can feel them crawling inside me, oozing with venom and sucking the life out of me..."*

What do you think?

Would you want to read on? I bet you do!

Guess what...

I spent not more than 5 minutes thinking, writing and editing those two headlines and two-first sentences.

You could argue that I've practiced and that's why it came so easy for me and I can turn around and say, EXACTLY!

I have practiced and I know what I'm talking about. So, when I tell you to abandon the misconception of the first line being your hook, listen to me. It's not as important because I can tell you right now that if the rest of your sentences suck, readers will abandon your book or article anyway.

So, don't waste your time trying to write the perfect first sentence. Work on **just writing** the first sentence, that's it.

You may focus on improving your first sentence during the editing phase.

Simple enough, right?

Awesome.

Let's talk about the characteristics of both my examples. If you break down both my first sentences, you would identify two things.

- I allowed my first sentence to shed more relevant and detailed information on the headline and title.

Why?

Because I already know that whoever opened my book or clicked on my article headline is baited. What he or she wants is more information. They want to satisfy their curiosity and the simplest and most practical thing to do is **give them more**. *"Give the people what they want!"*

- Give them what they want...but just a taste more!

I gave you a taste of information in the first sentences, enough to satisfy your initial curiosity but at the same time create a hunger for more. I wrote my sentences in a way that triggers more questions.

In the practical example, I introduced you to Mark and I revealed the reward of his weightloss being 6 pack abs. None of this unintentional. Many people who open weightloss and fitness articles are interested in body sculpting. The media and fitness industry have promoted an ideology that abs are the ultimate definition of sexiness and fitness.

I'm feeding off the readers desires. And I'm reeling him more and more with each sentences.

The exact same thing happened in my book's first sentence. The title piques curiosity about small creatures like cockroaches and insects (things that many people have a phobia for and some people are intrigued by) whereas my first sentence feeds off phobia's and fears and making the reader even more curious about what these crawlers are.

Why am I doing this? Good question.

Some may say it's because you want to keep people interested and curious throughout your book so that they stay invested. True as this may be, there's another reason which is more important.

It's about taking the reader on a journey.

Making the reader feel as if he is in the story and he's experiencing everything that the main character feels when discovering new things and facing new challenges. It's about making the reader enter the story, imagine what you want him to imagine and taking him or her on the most magical and enjoyable journey ever.

These 2 reasons are truly all that's holding you back - realistically speaking, of course. Every other reason all leads back to the biggest problem you may face - **fighting the war in your mind.**

You may or may not realize it but a lot of the problems you face as a writer are in your head. *And no, I'm not calling you crazy!*

What I mean is that the only thing holding you back from writing that first sentence and every other sentence is your insecurities, lack of discipline, laziness or fear. Heck, it could be every one of those reasons.

You are a writer. Period!

You are a writer when you decide to write. Nothing and nobody can stop you from being who you are meant to be - **a writer.**

The one exception and the only exception is **You.** You can be standing in your own way and if you are, it's time to embrace who you are and blossom into the artist you are meant to be.

Alot of people spend their entire lives being afraid.

Afraid that the path they want to be on is impossible. I'm here to tell you that it's not. The sooner you start, the sooner you can be on your way to accomplishing great things. My intention for writing this was to be as technical and practical as possible but what I realized is that the biggest setback and the most important hurdle to overcome is self-sabotage.

The only way to truly overcome self-sabotage is by delving into the world of positivity and motivation. I do hope you take me seriously when I say that you are meant to be whoever you dream of being.

Sometimes, it comes at the cost of hustling and facing fear but that's what living is about - **facing fear and failure head on and not being defeated.**

To write a book, you must be willing to embrace the writer within you and stop listening to that voice of doubt. Dig deeper and you'll hear a faint voice cheering you on, whispering words of wisdom and hope. **Listen to that voice!**

Let it guide you rather than the voice screaming in your face about failure. Ignore that douchebag!

Bottom Line: The first sentence is the reel, not the bait. Just have fun with it and write as you think. Don't worry about writing the perfect first sentence, there's no such thing. Leave the fine tuning for the editing phase. Step out of your comfort zone and ignore that voice of doubt and fear screaming at you. Focus on being you - a writer.

Wait, Take A Step Back...You Forgot About Planning (Aha!)

You're busy eating up everything I wrote about the first sentence but you didn't even think about how important planning is! *No gold star for you.*

Jokes aside, if you try to write as you think, you will have a hard time. (*You'll notice there's a section about writing as you think. It may seem counterintuitive but it's not. There's a system to follow. Planning is essential even when you want to wing it.*)

Let's avoid making writing any more difficult than it is.

Sad to say, I wasted a lot of time and energy writing books and articles that were half baked. In my head, they were amazing. But when it came time to translating my thoughts into words, it wasn't nearly as good as I envisioned.

Why?

Because I skipped a vital step.

Planning is an obligatory action. You absolutely cannot avoid it. I'm not even talking in-depth chapter analysis, I'm talking about a broad plan of your book ideas in the form of a mind map or linear points.

It takes not more than 30 minutes to get all your ideas down on paper but this simple act can save you hours of writing and vastly improve the quality of your end product.

Again, you already know this, don't you?

But, knowing something and applying it are two different things. It's not good enough to know what's right for you and not practice it. That's not how winning is done.

Let me tell you why...

You won't write an entire novel in one day. You just won't. That's why I named this 20K words in 4 days because it took me 4 separate days to write this. Planning is important because you will not be able to remember everything you were thinking and planning to write each time you open up your manuscript.

It's not like your brain pauses when you stop writing. Other experiences and thoughts take preference and your train of thought regarding an idea is easily swayed by the time a day passes.

You need a guide and that comes in the form of a written plan (*not typed, written*).

Debunking the myth of writers block

I remember a time, about 6 years ago, I was in school writing an English literature closed book paper that required all students to write a 500 word essay from the topics provided. It could be either fiction or non-fiction.

Regardless of whether a student hated writing or loved it, every student wrote their essay in the 1 hour 30 minutes provided. And yet on an ordinary day I find ample amount of writers who complain about writer's block.

It doesn't make sense!

I learnt something very important from this – people who complain about writer's block, including myself, **are full of shit.**

Not being able to write has nothing to do with an imaginative wall preventing your brain from turning ideas into words.

This is a myth.

Your inability to write is caused by 3 things:

1. Lack of certainty.
2. Lack of preparation.
3. Exhaustion.

These 3 things are why you can't write on any particular day. Showing up is not enough anymore. You know this and I bet you've struggled with this but showing up doesn't get the work done. You could show up and not write a single word for hours and chalk it down to writer's block but the fact remains is that you either lack certainty, lack preparation and/or you're exhausted.

It happens to the best of us but regardless of what advice you read and what your filthy lazy mind-set tells you, skipping the important steps of planning will cause the so-called 'writer's block'.

Lack of certainty.

I want you to imagine that I offered you one thousand dollars for you to write a 5000 word article on losing weight with a juice fast, would you be able to do it? Hell yes!

Heck, I think a homeless man on the street with little to no experience on writing would find it in him to complete the task. Why? Because of certainty. He know that at the end of 5000 words, there's a big cash reward waiting for him. More so than that, he knows with certainty what the topic is about.

Certainty is a sure thing and that certainty is what guarantees completion. If you want to write 20 thousand words in four days, you need to be absolutely certain on what your book is about. You ought to know, with certainty, how your story is going to play out.

Lack of Preparation

This is the big fish so I want you to pay careful attention. After you know for certain what your book is about and what your reason is for writing that particular book, **you need to prepare.**

And you would notice that I used the word **NEED**. It's obligatory and you cannot skip over preparation. If you do, you're going to have a 50% chance of failure.

What do you want? 100% certainty that you're going to write or 50%?

Anyway, preparation begins and ends by asking and answering one simple question – **WHY?**

I'm going to use an example to show you why you need to be asking why…

27 year old Jack died at 2:30pm when a bus crashed into his house and knocked him. – That's your topic/idea and you're certain about it. Now, here's where the preparation kicks in. You can't write thousands of words based off that one line. It's not enough! You need to flesh it out and the only way to do that is by asking why.

- **Why did a bus crash into Jack's house?** Because the driver lost control of the bus.
- **Why did the driver lose control of the bus?** Because he suffered from a heart attack while driving.

- **Why did he suffer from a heart attack?** Because he was overweight, stressed out and heart attacks ran in his family.

- **Why was Jack, a 27 year old, still at home at 2:30 in the afternoon?** He recently lost his job.

- **Why did he lose his job?** Because he covered for a co-worker who messed up on an important case.

- **Why did he cover for such co-worker?** Because he was in love with her.

I got all of that information by simply asking WHY and I could go on and on for hours until my small sentence turns into an entire map for the story.

Writing is simple if you don't skip over the fundamental actions. Too many writers are looking for the easy way out. They want to write a bestseller book without putting in the effort that bestselling authors are known for.

You will never be the best until you try to beat the best.

And that can only happen by emulating and improving on the actions successful writer's take.

Imagine if you expanded this step by asking more questions like HOW and WHEN. You could have every single detail needed to write an entire story without even needing a break.

Ironically, when you're certain about your idea, only then will you properly prepare. And when you prepare properly, you find more certainty. It's a cycle that makes writing simple.

Last but not least, Exhaustion.

I never thought for a moment that I would be advising writer's to take a break, especially since I gave you so much crap for being lazy, but I realized that exhaustion is not a state to mess around with.

It can destroy you and leave you completely drained of all motivation and consistency.

I can attest to this because after being diagnosed with psoriatic arthritis, exhaustion and fatigue plagued me like an SOB.

Regardless of how certain I was and the amount of prep I completed, I was unable to write due to sheer exhaustion.

During this time, and only this time, I urge you to stop and sleep or meditate. Don't do anything besides those two things because I don't want you forming a new unhealthy or lazy habit. I want you to program your mind to associate sleep from exhaustion as a means of furthering your goals as a writer.

Rest is okay – it's even important. You cannot find the light for the dark blankness when your eyes and brain register nothing but exhaustion.

What Makes Writing Fun For Me

Don't give up reading this book just because I'm about to yap away about what I like. I know, I promised to focus on YOU but I guarantee this section will be worth your time.

Whilst writing this, I was listening to a song but initially I thought that focussing over an epic song will distract me. To my surprise, even with music blasting in my ears and my feet tapping on the ground melodically, the words flew out of me like water through a filter – clean and concentrated.

I swear to god that when I write in silence, I struggle. It's weird because I simply can't multitask to save my life AND I personally hate and disapprove of multitasking but in this case, **it works superbly**.

However, the main point of this section is that when you fuse leisure with work, you find a balance that allows you to work at optimum.

Believe me when I say that this is the most ideal state and situation to be writing in. If you ever find yourself uncharacteristically writing so smoothly and easily, **keep going and don't stop**. When you're out of juice, think about what you were doing or where you were that is different than normal. That difference will be your key to limitless fun with writing.

You can cheerfully say goodbye to those dreadful work hours and build a routine of writing whilst having a blast.

I like to write in style. With music playing, windows wide open and fresh air smashing against my face, sun or rain seeping through the light thin curtains and all my sticky notes from prep laid out across the table for me as reference. And for the sake of it, I put on sunglasses to give me that extra cool vibe.

Let me tell you something…This routine makes me feel so good inside and I have so much fun. I feel the words inside coursing through my veins begging to be plastered onto the digital paper on the computer screen.

I think the reason music works so well, not only in helping make the process of writing fun and easy but in inspiring ideas, is because musicians and artists put a lot of creative effort into writing and composing music. So, when you fuel your own desire to create art whilst enjoying another form of art simultaneously, it's almost as if that artist is guiding you to unleash that creative genius within you.

Movies, books, poems, podcasts and even pictures can serve the same purpose of music.

Heck, nature or even man-designed environments could do it for you. This may be a bad example since gaming on its own is so fun but when gamers struggle to conquer a difficult boss, they find cheat codes or patterns in gaming which allow them to bypass irritating or monotonous gameplay.

What I'm telling you to do is find your cheat codes and patterns as a writer that make things easier, faster and smoother.

The most influential factor is your mind-set.

Many people get into writing motivated by the prospect of making money or gaining fame. There's nothing wrong with that. In fact, it works. You will feel motivated. Every day I see a notification on Facebook from new authors promoting their newly self-published books.

I take the time to browse through most of these authors work as a token of my support and I admire that many took the leap of faith and tried. It shows enthusiasm and a drive to try something new which I find to be admirable. That's a good mind-set.

However, I notice a mistake amongst many of these authors. Like me, they decided to write and publish solely for those motivating factors. They searched online for advice, discovered niche marketing and publishing, threw together a 25 - 30 page book and published it on Amazon Kindle with the hopes of earning money.

It pains me to say this but that state of being, that mind-set, it's build on a very flimsy foundation that will break when the results aren't good.

Writing is an art.

It's a form of expressing yourself. Done correctly, what you write will outlive you.

Don't you want to leave behind a legacy to be remembered by? Are you sure a 30 page, low quality, money making book is what you want to leave behind under your name? Because I'll tell you what, it's not worth it.

I'm speaking from experience and as I write this, I have the strongest urge to delete all my slap dash books from Amazon and start from scratch.

Writing is fun when you start to think of it as a part, an extension, of you. Physically, mentally and spiritually. I'm making the conscious decision to approach writing with the same commitment and dedication I do to eating food.

I want to be hungry to create the most appealing, tantalizing, mouth-watering piece of art I can each and every day. I want to challenge myself and test the extent of my abilities. I want to inspire you to change your mind-set and be the support you need in going from 0 words to thousands a day.

Adopt a similar mind-set. Put yourself in the shoes of a 10 year old kid who gets to play video games every day. Regardless of how long he plays, he'll never get tired of playing the game. At times, a particular game may grow boring for him but he'll try a new one until he can go back.

You can be a kid again. All you have to do is change the way you think.

I'll leave you with the great words of Tony Robbins – "*The brain isn't programmed for happiness. It's programmed for survival.*" You have to be the force who reprograms your brain to prioritize happiness over logistics.

Essential Writing Tips

I remember being criticized by a reviewer who said that I should be the NIKE guy in the world of writing because all she got from my book was *JUST DO IT!*

To be honest, I was completely baffled. Such a radically conflicting reaction to my book. I had people joining my email list and emailing me about how much I helped them improve their word count and yet this individual found little value in my book.

What messed with my head was the fact that I actually put in a significant amount of thought and effort into that book unlike the rest.

I wasn't sure whether to laugh in disbelief or cry in disappointment.

Needless to say, that piece of criticism is the reason behind this section. I am going to provide you with essential writing tips and some of it will be technical in nature. I want no reader to feel the way that individual did. And I give you my word that I will not waste your time on stuff you already know unless refreshing your memory is important.

1. Write The Way You Can

There's a misconception amongst writers that in order to write a book, you must possess a vocabulary bank and mastery of storytelling. That is incorrect.

To write a book you must simply write. Whether such book is good or bad is of no concern during the writing stage.

We spoke about this earlier but the individual stages of writing ought not to overlap. When they do, often it leads to unnecessary pit stops and a destruction of productivity.

You don't have to emulate Stephen King. Granted, being able to write as consistently and as brilliantly as him would be an enormous accomplishment, but you don't have to. If anything, what you should be focussing on is finding a voice you're comfortable and successful with.

The best way to do this is by writing frequently in the way you can. It means experimenting and letting your chapters construct themselves in the manner you're capable off right now.

Improvement is vital and I encourage every writer to strive for mastery but when you're starting out or if you're attempting to increase your word count, the best way to achieve those goals is by focussing on just writing the way you can.

The first draft of any book is flawed. However, having a first draft means that your story, from start to finish, has been realized and completed. Only at this point should you begin to edit and attempt to improve your writing sentence by sentence.

Patience is not my strong point but if I can do it, anyone can.

Enter with the intention of writing the best book ever but act on such intention in stages. During the planning stage, go nuts and implement your intention. During the writing stage, just write without criticism. During the editing stage, go nuts again and try to improve every sentence until you're satisfied.

Sure, perfection is not attainable but improvement is. With each and every book you will get better. Words will flow smoother and writing won't be such a daunting task. You'll meet word quotas and you'll pick up on flaws faster.

For the reviewer who left me that piece of criticism, this section is for you. If you want to write more words, start by writing what you can and not what you wish you could. If you're not at a Stephen king level, write at the level you're at and work up to editing like Stephen king until your work is of that standard. You'll realize that your capabilities as a writer will automatically improve through self-editing.

And that's a very important point. Self-editing, though daunting, is an incredibly effective way to improve your skills as a writer. It takes a lot of strength and commitment to look at your own work through critical eyes. If you manage to do that, you'll be walking on sunshine.

Essentially…JUST DO IT!

Being natural entails writing the way you think and speak whilst implementing a few natural conversational elements into your writing.

For instance, I speak out loud when writing. Doing this allows me to identify when I sound like a damn robot or suave like a Don Juan.

If I like how I sound, I'll like how I write just as much.

This is such a simple tip but it produces results. Perhaps you already know this but knowing something and being conscious of it when working is two different things.

Now let's talk about those natural conversational elements. Many authors get flabbergasted and frustrated when writing dialogue. Some are better than others but being able to write dialogue that flows naturally isn't as easy as it sounds.

I want to touch on 3 essentials:

1. Interruptions
2. Use of slang words
3. Variation of length

Notice that when having a conversation in person, people interrupt each other. Either through agreement, disapproval, argumentatively, rudely or informatively.

I'll use an argumentative example:

"Put the gun down right now or else I'll–"

"Or else what? What are you gonna do, Pete? Beat me like you did to Jessie?" interrupted Rick.

As you can see, Rick interrupted Pete mid-sentence. Someone in a heated argument isn't going to be polite and wait for the opposing party to deliver his dialogue unchallenged.

Human beings are unpredictable. And as a writer, you have to predict the unpredictable by putting yourself in the shoes of each character.

This takes time and investment but if you planned your story and characters with certainty, you'll have no issue writing appropriate dialogue for them and knowing how unpredictable they are.

Also take note of the slang used in the above dialogue (*gonna – going to*). It was natural and expected from someone in an argument. Do you think you would be concerned of your tense or sentence construction when trying to blast someone to smithereens? I don't think so.

Last but not least, size does not matter – no pun intended. Sentences that are constructed with a specific word count are monotonous. Quite a while back I read something along the lines of comparing writing with music. Let each sentence sing a new tune. It could be just a few words. It could be a barrage of words smashed together that creates sweet, melodious music that resonates within your soul.

People speak without a word count in mind. Their sentences vary in length. So yes, comparing writing and sentence construction to music is apt.

3. Write As You Feel

Finding your voice as a writer is not as complicated as it sounds. On the contrary, all you need to do is write regularly and experiment.

But, how does one do that?

Well, for starters, write according to how you feel about a particular event. Note that I didn't ask you to write according to how you felt in the moment but how you felt about that story line. You see, one chapter could be buzzing with positivity and the story line could be in sync with that. The hero is amongst family, he's living life with no worries and his goal to conquer the magical world is alive and burning bright.

Write your story quirkily, happily, relaxed and light. It fits the chapter. Maybe the main character is reserved and very driven. Perhaps he values his goal more than he does his own life. In that case, you could write with tones of nobility, vigour and seriousness.

However, when our hero is dealt a bad set of cards, your tone of writing can instantly change and so can your voice.

And this brings me to a very important point – your voice as a writer is susceptible to your manipulation. In fact, browse through my first chapter of this book and you'll find I took on a much less academic voice as I have now.

This is perfect. Consistency is the key to success but not at the expense of quality. If you consistently adopt a failing voice, your chances of it succeeding are slim. But, if you play around and let your voice be influenced by emotions, things become much clearer and just like composing music, your book will be a rainbow of colorful voices.

A writer who is capable of crafting his words in an enjoyable fashion will impress his readers far more than a boring academic robot spewing jargon onto a page.

Funnily enough, I worked with an author once who considered his book to be THE BEST and when reading it (*or rather, trying to read it*), you would be blown away by his mastery of the English language. It looked as if this book was dug up from medieval times when writers wrote for a breed of readers far different than our generation.

As a writer, he did a great job of using the English language but unfortunately, he wrote for maybe 100 people from the 1500's in a world of 7 billion people. I kid you not. You would require a dictionary by your side and someone to guide you along page by page. I am a law student and none of the textbooks and sources I've ever read come close to being as complicated as this author's book.

I don't know if it was an arrogant attempt to write like a 1500's professor or something entirely else but no normal reader would want to read that book.

This is the last thing you want to do – especially if you're trying to convey an important message to readers. In the beginning of this book I told you to focus on effectively transferring your ideas into the brain of your readers. Essentially, make them think what you want them to think in the best manner possible.

This author didn't abide by this rule and he ended up with a book that's worthy only of stroking his ego instead of shaping the world with a valuable message.

This stigma attached to writer's being arrogant is one to avoid. You are the provider and it is your job to feed those hungry for information the best possible source of food. It is your duty! Don't ever think that you are better than your readers!

Respect them as they deserve to be.

4. Identify 1 Person And Satisfy All His/Her Expectations

I learnt this little tip from a guy named Dewan and it helped me tremendously. It is easier to write when knowing exactly who you want reading your book than to try and please everybody.

Some authors write for themselves. You are a person, right? I hope you are. And you have likes as well as dislikes. So, if you write a book for yourself, you're essentially identifying a target audience that resembles you.

If you can write a book that you'd be extremely satisfied with as a reader then you can target people just like you and quadruple your rate of success.

It's a lot easier to do this than to write for everyone.

Not everyone agrees with each other and not everyone thinks the same way. If that were so, we wouldn't be living in a war torn world. We wouldn't be consuming GM foods or destroying the ozone layer.

Broadly speaking, non-fiction readers want facts. They want information that can be used and relevant in the real world.

Fiction readers on the other hand want to be entertained. When reading a book, they want to be spellbound and enticed by all the creativity and emotive storytelling.

Being conscious of this will drastically impact your mind-set moving forward. I know of many readers who complain about fluff and with good reason. When a writer is unprepared or dabbling, he or she tends to stray from their goal.

Just remind yourself that you are writing for someone important. You want to provide that person with everything they desire and take action on that want.

5. The 3 Arc Formula

Do you struggle with the flow of your book? Perhaps you have all these ideas in your head but can't seem to construct them into a proper story when it's time to write.

It's not just you – most writer's when starting out and even seasoned writers encounter this problem.

Guess what…the solution is awfully simple and you've seen it at least a hundred times.

Quite recently I watched Ride Along. Not the best movie in the world but a typical one nonetheless. The story begins with Ice Cube doing what he does best, kicking ass and being a hard-core cop. Kevin Hart's character is living life along the same lines except he kicks ass in games and is happily engaged to Ice Cube's sister in the movie.

All is well!

Everything starts off great until the story progresses and shit hits the fan. Ice Cube is betrayed by his colleagues, a killer drug lord makes his appearance in a warehouse with a bunch of criminals and Kevin Hart gets one attempt to save Ice Cube.

However, somehow, the two heroes manage to escape this dangerous encounter with an injury only to find that their beloved is being held hostage by the main antagonist.

They rush over, kick ass and save the day. The movie ends on a positive, happy go lucky and funny note.

Ride Along used the 3 arc formula. Grow a tree, set it on fire, save it or let it burn. In this case, they saved the tree.

Essentially, start your story depicting things to either be good, light and easy or slightly bad and mundane. Focus on the lives of your main characters and give your readers a chance to appreciate what normal feels like.

Just when your readers and characters seem to be enjoying the normalcy of life, plunge them into danger. In other words, set the tree alight. Let everything go to hell and place your characters in a state of turmoil.

Finally, after intense battles and desperation, save the tree by saving the day or letting it burn to the ground.

I read about this in the book - *From 2K to 10K Words A Day* – phenomenal stuff and I would encourage anyone to give it a read.

People are generally uncomfortable with change.

A filthy rich person would be terribly uncomfortable if they lost all their money. Conversely, in a twisted story that we see happen in real life too many times, an abused woman in a marriage is afraid of change even if the change could be good for her.

In other words, trauma has become normal for her and fear for her life is something she lives with.

Her assailant becomes a norm – an anchor.

So even turmoil can be regarded as normal in your story.

The tree set alight could be her freedom from this man when he gets arrested for armed robbery.

Her battle could be about embracing the change of freedom and happiness. Just when she overcomes her fears and accepts her new found freedom to live as she pleases, the man returns and with that, the burning tree disintegrates into ashes.

Good – Bad – Good.

Bad – Good – Bad.

The tree represents the core element of the story. In the example above, her abusive relationship is what's set on fire. The tree represents the core element that the story is built around.

Removing it and changing it results in unexpected events.

Understanding this concept can make your life far easier as a writer.

This may not be a rule but most commercially successful books follow the 3 arc approach. Go with the flow or discover a system that best suits your story. The choice is yours!

I'm an instincts kind of guy.

I go with my gut feeling. If a particular arc feels good to me, I write it. Yes, I'm a crazy simpleton (contrasting but you get the idea, right?).

However, outlining is a skill that makes writing pleasant. It really does. Personally, I find it boring but it's usually the boring stuff that produces good results.

Think about it.

A boring diet is usually aligned with a fit body. I'm a huge Daredevil fan and actor Charlie Cox honed his physique by exercising properly and eating a boring diet consisting of chicken, broccoli and sweet potato.

Not very enticing items, am I right?

But they produce spectacular results.

An outline is simple. Well, it should be simple. Imagine that your book is a movie and you've just watched it at your favourite cinema.

The movie is fresh in your head and it's your job to give an outline and breakdown of the plot, characters and main happenings. Scratch that, it's not your ~~job~~, it's your hobby!

Hobbies are fun. Happiness and positivity are usually attached to a hobby. Never will you find someone in a dreadful mood doing something they willingly chose to do for the sake of enjoyment.

Outlining can be fun.

Once you've outlined everything important and essential, start fleshing out the details of each critical event to the plot and the lead characters. You can divide your notes between different time lines such as the past, present and future.

By doing this, you can sketch a basic backstory for both the main plot and characters.

It's the principle behind outlining that matters. What you are trying to establish is a firm understanding of non-negotiable events. The outline is a guide. It's to prevent you from writing out of sync whilst keeping you on a consistent track.

It also clears up space in your head for new ideas. Trying to juggle your entire plot, minute details and writing all in your head is silly. That's a recipe for burnout.

Writers have even used outlines to overcome writers block. What I strongly urge you to do is complete every outline on paper by hand.

You can enter it onto a document in the future but your initial outlining MUST always happen on paper.

The Nitty Gritty

Sensei is ready to level up your word count. I wrecked my brain trying to decide whether or not it would be smart of me to set out a system for you.

The obvious answer is **yes!**

That's exactly why you purchased the book.

The problem, however, is that no system is a One-Size-Fits-All. It became my problem to figure out how to optimize things for a wide variety of readers. I want you, Pablo, Sizwe, Stephanie, Ali, Kurosaki Ichigo and everyone else to thrive as writers.

I will consider this book a complete failure if you ended (or abandoned) reading what I've written because it didn't offer you sustainable and realistic advice.

Bearing that in mind, let's go over a few ways you can push out 20 thousand words in 4 days.

You have a few choices:

- Write 5000 words a day. No more, no less.
- You set a minimum word count of 500 words every hour for 10 hours.
- Write 1000 words at 5 different intervals.

- Write as much as you can in as many hours per day as you can.

What I have decided to do is share my formula and discuss a variety of ways you can find and use time sparingly to meet your word count deadlines.

Which brings me to my first daily ritual –

I set a deadline for the day.

I am a writer. For the rest of my life, I will be a writer. Regardless of the fact that I will be a qualified lawyer at the end of 2016, I am a writer first. Which means that writing is my priority. I can sit the all day for the next 30 years at my computer screen churning out page after page.

Perhaps you can't do that.

Just like me, you may have goals right now and other expectations requiring attention.

But, what I've learnt over time is that time-management begins by actually managing time. The ability to sit your behind down for 5 minutes and pen down how much time you want to spend on each activity and what your goals are for the day is critical.

Time mastery may be the defining factor in whether you will be successful or not. And I'm not hyping it up more than it is. This is a fact.

My goal is to write 5000 words every day before 12:30pm. Since I start my morning at 8:30am, which gives me 4 hours to write 5000 words.

It takes no math genius to figure out that 1250 words every hour can do the job. But, life is unpredictable and whether or not you can work at such a programmed state.

Sometimes I finish a 1000 words in 35 minutes. Instead of shutting down for the next 25 minutes, I take a few minute off and jump right back in. I finish early on some days whereas on other days I clock in just in time.

Then there are days when I pass the 4 hour mark without meeting my deadline. I soldier on and make sure that I at least meet my word count.

This sets me back a bit but I cut down on some leisure time to make up for it.

Believe it or not, I reduced the time I spend watching TV and I now have 2 hours more to play around with.

So, before you get started writing, think about all the mundane activities you partake in daily and try to reduce time spent on them. I didn't say quit altogether, just reduce and spend that saved time productively.

To be the best, you have to know what you're good and bad at. On average, I can type up to 69 words per minute. Not bad at all given that I would only clock in at 20 words or so when I started writing professionally years ago.

Also, I have psoriatic arthritis. Yeah, I know, it sucks! But, we have to work with what we have and this painful inflamed joints are what I have. Yet, I'm still able to maintain my word count because I know for a fact that there is no pain without gain.

Nevertheless, to help motivate me and keep me on track, I print out a monthly goal and word count calendar. The funny thing about people is that they read things in books like this but never actually complete the activities recommended.

I want you to do exactly what I tell you to do. If I say print out a calendar to keep track of your daily word count, you do it!

If I tell you to go outside and meditate in the sun naked, you do it! Okay, maybe not...

Anyway, do the activities, okay? Authors include them because they're relevant and they work. I can guarantee that any smart and hardworking author would never include unnecessary work for their readers.

When you find activities in a book, always be conscious of the fact that they were strategically planned for your benefit.

Learning is an active task. The more you engage yourself, the better you understand things. With understanding comes learning and mastery.

Keep a track of all the words you write on a calendar. To grow requires awareness of who you are, what you are capable of doing and what you have done.

Note: *When you sign up to my newsletter, I'll send you a 2 books on writing as well as a printable word count calendar. And yes… I am Santa clause!*

Believe it or not, I watched my mother write a 15000 word fiction story, from conception to completion, in just a week. She must have spent no more than 10 hours on the actual writing process itself.

She was able to accomplish such a feat by applying herself in pursuit of completion.

One highly important characteristic a writer must possess is an obsession with completion. I witness my mother dive into tasks on a daily basis and without flinching at the enormous scope of work that these things require. Her most admirable quality being her obsession with completion. It is the reason for all her success and accomplishments.

Too many of us spend life giving in too little and expecting too much. We want fame without having to hustle for it. We want loads of money without creating books that are of a high standard. We want publishers to invest in us without providing anything more than substandard work.

Why?

Why are we so hell bent on taking the easy route for everything important in life?

I ask you this question and beg of you to give me an answer. **Why do we sabotage our future?**

Writing is not a tool for money. **It is a tool for self-expression!** Money is just a by-product that is rewarded to those who try their best to express themselves in the best light possible.

The main reason I spoke about my mother in this book is because she wrote her story by hand. Unlike 99% of people, including myself, she opted to write the old fashioned way. And yet still, writers complain that it's too hard to write even with computers and audio programs that easily transcribe recordings into words.

How foolish and lazy of a generation we are!

Writing 20 thousand words or 200 thousand words requires no more than hard work. You can spend months trying to figure out how to write faster but you will never complete a book unless you are willing to put in the time and effort required.

This is not an easy career choice.

Dedication and hard work cannot be substituted for hacks and tricks. You want to write more words? Well, make more time to write. Better yet, use your time better. Get in more words every hour by planning more.

Learn and pile on as much information until you reach a level of mastery on a topic. For instance, writing a fiction book is dependent on the source material in your head and on paper. The scope of such books are so enormous that finding the right idea to start with is like a brutal mission.

So, what do you do? Embark on that brutal mission and waste time? No! Instead, use your time better by writing down all your ideas, plots, subplots, background stories and so on. Higher word counts and better books are the result of better planning.

Another useful tip is to write in segments. We spoke about the 3 Arc formula applied to your story as a whole but the very same formula can be used in each chapter. Writing fiction is like solving a puzzle. Solve portions of a puzzle until they combine and create an entire image.

Writing can be seen as the same. You could take your readers on a journey from A to Z or you could throw strategically what seems like random letters until what you have spells the word 'AWESOME'.

Time Management? Hmm...

I've written many books about time management. Most of them detail ways in which prioritizing tasks can help boost your productivity. I go on and on about things to do and not to do. But, in this moment, I feel like it was a waste of time.

Granted, people who read it enjoyed what I chose to share with them. Perhaps it even benefited my readers.

What irks me is that my books are a reflection of myself. They're an extension of me. And I don't like what I see. I shouldn't be searching for hacks or shortcuts to find more time in my day. I shouldn't need to.

If writing is my dream and becoming a bestselling author is an item on my bucket list, I should be dedicating as much time as I need to accomplish it. I shouldn't be working my schedule around gaming, TV shows and socializing.

I should be working on my dream as much as possible.

20 thousand words in 4 days? It's a great number. In fact, it's a superb number.

But, 20 thousand words in 2 days is better.

If I'm truly committed and dedicated to this craft, I should be more than willing to meet that goal. I should be writing every chance I get. And when I'm not writing, I should be researching.

If you have made it this far, I want you to be honest with yourself and answer this. *Are you willing to give everything to meet this goal?* Mathematically and scientifically, it's more than possible to write 20 thousand words in 4 days.

What it comes down to is whether or not you are driven and strong minded. If you aren't, it's time you become the person and writer you need to be.

It's time to start...

Right now.

Grab a page and write down these following words - "*I will write 20 thousand words in 4 days. I will not fail.*"

Good. Now you've brought your thoughts into the real world. It's time for you to bring your best cards to the table.

If you were to stop watching TV shows and movies for the next 4 days, if you were to limit your social media usage and if you were to wake up an extra hour earlier to write, how much time can you save and dedicate to writing?

Work it out and get started. It's time to forget all the productivity tips and spend your day doing what you want to do.

I know people will give me slack for writing this as if I expect you to abandon your day job to write. Believe me when I say that I completely understand what it feels like to work in an office for a demanding boss and coming home exhausted to do chores.

I've walked in those very same shoes.

But, if you really want to do this and you aren't looking for some magical secret sauce, then I guarantee that you can do it.

Nothing will hold you back...

Not even your own insecurities.

Researching Is A Pain…Nope! Not Anymore

No matter how much I tried to understand the art of research, I just couldn't bring myself to enjoy it.

As a freelance writer, I get tasked with unusual jobs. Some topics baffle me to the point of wanting to pull my hair off.

I get tired.

Bored.

Definitely annoyed.

But, after balling my eyes out like an anime character, it hits me.

My fingers start to move across the keyboard and pick up speed as sentences manifest one after the other.

It becomes easier and I start writing as fast as I think.

Fascinatingly, I start thinking faster too.

From spending hours in agony researching about some product I may never use in my entire life, I get to this point of forming opinions about it and excitedly whipping up benefit after benefit from all its features.

I transition from an annoyed writer to a lifelong fan of the product.

Suddenly, I'm 800 or a 1500 words in and I'm amazed at the stellar article staring back at me.

"How? How is this possible?" I ask myself time and time again even though I know the reason.

I learnt.

All that dreadful research did the trick.

It gave me enough knowledge to understand unknown concepts, apply them to real life scenarios, compare them to other concept and craft my own ideas.

I simply learned everything I could through research.

Whether it be from an article, video or podcast, research is by far the most useful tool a writer can possess.

If you can find it within yourself to put in the work to learn more, you won't have such a hard time writing long form articles and chapters upon chapters of your book.

You may even love writing on the topic you hated not more than 2 hours ago.

Research may be a pain but it's a critical tool used for writing. And you know what, doing the research could save the writing process from becoming dreadful.

We spoke about this earlier but research is best done by asking these questions:

- Why?
- How?
- When?
- What?
- For Who?

Anything can be learned, even in a short space of time by working with what you have. Start from the bottom. Analyze the simplest of concepts and further your knowledge question by question.

Overlapping Ideas

A few years ago I was at the Mall with my best friend on our way to watch a movie. For the life of me I can't remember which movie we watched that day but I do remember updating him on all the plans I had for my fictional novel.

There was a particular idea that excited me and I wanted it to be an incredibly important factor in my story.

I was pumped.

Everything was falling into place and my story was turning into what I consider a masterpiece.

Anyway, we picked up some popcorn and coke, proceeded into the cinema, squeezed our way through the poorly designed isles and dropped our slightly arrogant asses onto the seats.

The movie began and about half way into it, this almost insignificant and overshadowed scene played out. Nevertheless, the movie finished and we exited the cinema but something was bugging me. I just couldn't put my finger on it.

As the two of us walked outside airing our thoughts about the movie, it hit me like a thunder bolt from hell.

That small scene in the movie is based on the idea I had for my book!

I felt like shit!

The entire time I tried to wrap my head around it but without a doubt, it was the same.

No way could I go with that idea anymore and my story would have to be overhauled. What a nightmare.

I made an attempt but failed.

Before long, the story I worked so hard on was abandoned.

My poor baby (lol).

I'm so damn disappointed. If only I wasn't as naive back then. But, everything happens for a reason and I learned a valuable lesson.

Ideas overlap.

Sometimes, an idea of yours may have drastic similarities to other stories. But that's okay. You're still allowed to use it as long as you had no intention to infringe someone else's copyright.

As long as you're not stealing someone else's idea or claiming to be the mastermind behind a particular 'discovery', it's okay. Don't abandon your book.

Books and stories will have similarities. Ideas will overlap but it's no excuse for you to throw your work away.

Don't get me wrong.

Writing a story about a young wizard named Barry Lotter whose parents were killed by an evil wizard whose name shall not be spoken will get you a copyright suit. Or so I think. However, writing a book about wizards and an evil wizard is not a copyright infringement.

Am I making sense?

You aren't going to get sued from the makers of Jumper for writing a story about teleporting. It doesn't work that way.

So, the next time you have an idea that turns out to overlap with another book, don't chuck it before making certain that it's not copyright infringement and whether or not it really is the same.

Start your book on wizards, don't just abandon it because a Harry Potter exists. You can do something just as good or even better!

As long as you are the maker of your story and you are invested, don't abandon it.

The Throw Up Method

Writing is easy.

We've figured that out. What's difficult is thinking. What's more difficult is thinking and trying to write with hands that are plagued with arthritis. Trust me, it's painful as hell.

But, that has never stopped me from writing daily and this technique will help you do the same.

I call it the throw up method of writing many words in any amount of time. You can take anywhere between 2 to 6 hours to write 5000 words in a day but the plain and simple fact is that this method works.

You will churn out every bit of content you have floating in your brain until there's nothing but dust and rusty old cogs needing a good oiling and some TLC.

Nevertheless, sometimes I start a brand new book without much planning and write everything that comes to mind on that topic. Whether it directly or indirectly related, whether it's relevant in today's time or not, whether I like what I'm writing or not, I just let the words flow out of me and I throw it all up onto my screen.

At the end, it looks like a massive rainbow cake without any structure.

But, I write far more words without suffering. What I usually do afterwards is start peeling the surface away. By this, I mean that I remove all the junk and fluff. I pick out those paragraphs and sections of content that make sense and are worthy of using.

When I do this, I divide these chapters into a few pages.

Each upcoming day I'll dedicate an hour to each idea and write as much as I possibly can. In other words, I throw up more detailed content on a particular idea. I do this over and over again until I find myself with a completed book that is in desperate need for editing.

BUT...

I have a book.

And it's complete.

Which means that I beat 99% of people who talk about writing and plan on it but never get down to doing it.

Sure, this is not the best technique for writing a best seller but right now our interest is not in bestselling status but in writing more words daily.

More importantly, it's about writing faster and not killing yourself from the sheer frustration of not knowing how to get started.

Would you believe me If I told you that what you're reading right now, this entire section, this sentence too, was not planned at all.

I didn't make any notes on paper nor did I do any research besides the 10 minutes it took for me to think about this undiscovered method that lay dormant in my mind. It went unnoticed for so long until I realized my own actions were aligned with this very same method of writing.

Many times I used the throw up method to snap out of the comfort zone and writer's block!

Perhaps we spend far too much time focusing on what we wish we could write rather than what we are capable of writing right now.

Improvement is an essential goal for every writer but the fundamental tool used for improving is simply writing and thinking faster.

Can it be done?

Yes.

Am I still being the Nike ambassador?

No.

I don't believe so.

I've provided you with enough principles and ideas to craft your skills and talents. It's up to you now on what you do with the advice in this book. You could simply read it and let it collect dust at the back of your brain or you could act on it and learn.

The best form of learning is through self-testing.

If I were to sit you down right now and asked you to ask and answer 5 questions about your book, how well would you score? Would you be able to narrate a summary or overall outline of your story to me right now or would you fumble to piece together something worthwhile?

Struggling with self-designed questions on content you ought to know is just solid proof that you don't have a solid understanding of your story or article. Without having the information in your mind, there's absolutely no way you can pen a book on that topic.

You will give up before you even make it onto chapter 5.

All I need from you is two things:

- Research everything related to your topic before you even think about writing.

- Write as much as you can without thinking about editing or the nitty gritty. (*Yip, for those who get stuck in the planning loop, this 'counterintuitive' technique is for YOU!*)

This entire technique is built on a lack of technique. What does this mean? Well, it means that you should pay no attention to your skills, techniques and abilities to write during the writing phase but just focus on pushing out the thoughts in your head onto paper.

Regardless of whether or not it makes sense or whether you like what's being written or not, you just focus on throwing up every bit of related information onto the screen.

Get it?

Good.

Now try it.

After you finish up, take a break, start chipping away and edit until what you have is usable.

The more you do this, the better you get at writing faster. Soon, it will become second nature to you and writing itself will be easier, thoughts will flow faster and you'll go about starting and finishing a book without a hassle.

The Art Of Movement

Why do we write?

What was the reason for people to write for the last 2000+ years? It couldn't have been for just fame or money. Neither could be for a feeling of satisfaction or a means of passing time by.

Writing is aligned with movement.

Everything in this world that is alive is in a constant state of motion. Nothing remains the same forever and everything moves from one point to the other.

Anything that stagnates for too long gets left behind and eventually forgotten.

Which is why people over all these years wrote. They wanted to see an idea progress and move. Not only from the past and into the future but to see the idea itself move and adapt.

Writers are the Gods of their own stories. They write the destiny of every character in a book.

Imagine being in control of free will?

Having the ability to throw certain events at characters that you created and then giving them a choice to make that you as the creator get to decide.

That is what writing is about.

A desire to see movement.

I had the idea of writing 20K words in 4 days. I wanted to witness this idea being moved from my brain onto paper and into your brain. But, the desire to watch the idea itself move from me to you comes with the expected movement towards change.

You have the ability to absorb and use information in a light that fits your story. The power of movement means that you may adapt and move my ideas into a new direction that works in a completely different or similar way.

This movement is constant and it will never die.

The next time you decide to write a chapter that has been bugging you for weeks or months, think about where you want your characters to move in their life. Write about how they moved from one idea to another, from one decision to another, from one phase to another.

Falling in love is movement. Similarly, falling out of love is movement too. Buying a gun is a movement, both mentally and emotionally. It changes the tone in which the story moves and gives the character a host of decisions to make and ways to move that are all brand new.

One movement triggered a host of new possible movement.

You, the writer, the god of your story, have complete control over what happens and in which direction things move.

Use that power however you so wish.

It's yours, after all.

Needless to say, the art of movement will help you move forward.

The Challenge

Have you ever found yourself being challenged by someone better than you on something you're not proficient at?

In many cases, you either quit before starting or you embrace the challenge with open arms. When you do, a sense of pride is established and your desire to defeat the competition and destroy the challenge flares up.

It is during these phases when you outperform yourself and others.

Why?

It's not because of some miracle or a fluke.

Some may argue it has something to do with luck. I get it. I agree. But luck doesn't factor into the equation when the writer himself or herself has nothing noticeable to show.

Luck is just an extra boost across the finish line.

For the entire race, everything that you accomplish and all the hurdles you overcome is strictly due to your abilities.

Your hard work, your dedication and your desire to win.

Winning is what separates winners from losers.

That strong, burning desire to win is what fuels your abilities. Our minds are very susceptible to influence. As we get older, negative influence has a stronger impact on our brains. We begin to fester a sense of negativity with each bad encounter until we damage a thought process that unfortunately drops us into the losing category.

The only way to break free and unleash the giant within you is to grab a challenge by the horns and give it your best shot with the intention of winning.

I always believe that my lack of luck is covered by my excessive input of work. Where other authors may succeed from a lucky novel, I may write a 100 books until I acquire the same results.

I've accepted that as my challenge.

If it means me actually writing a 100 books, I'll do it.

Quitting because I have no luck is a silly reason. It's a foolish reason.

I want you to challenge yourself to take whichever route is open for you. If luck is not on your side, take up the challenge of working 10 times as hard as any other author to achieve your dreams.

Yes, it will be difficult.

Perhaps you'll wake up some mornings questioning whether anything will work out. I have fears of being a struggling author all my life when I could simply settle for being a lawyer and living on a comfortable set salary.

I could easily do that.

But I won't.

If there's something to be afraid off, then there's something incredible to be gained from winning.

Doubt has no room in the mind of a writer. It deserves no attention and comfort from you. When it appears, do what it's trying to make you refrain from doing – this applies to important things like your goals and dreams.

I challenge you.

Face your fears head on and abandon the notion of luck if it's not meant for you. If you have to be like me and work 10 times harder than other authors, do it.

If this is the path we have been dealt, let's run on it until we catch up with those who were gifted a lucky path.

Yes, the path taken may incredibly differ but the destination is the same.

You and I may have to hustle and write until our brains are mush and our fingers are worn out. But, we'll do it.

Why?

Because we have a desire to win. We don't walk away from a challenge and if it means staying awake until the wee hours of the morning to crack a script, we'll do it!

That's how winning is done!

A lucky path may exist, the damn hard path exists but there's absolutely no such things as the easy way.

It doesn't exist.

Anyone who tells you otherwise is a fool.

The best things in life are earned from hard work.

Be the underdog if you have to but get the job done. You want to write 20000 words in 4 days, set the challenge. Set a goal, make a plan, drop all your time-wasting activities, work until you literally collapse onto the bed but *'Just Do It'*!

Don't get me wrong, writing may not be fun at all. It could even become the most tiring and daunting task ever. Granted, it doesn't have to be that way but when it becomes that way, we push on and we do what needs to be done.

I'll say it again – that's how winning is done!

To the reviewer who criticized me for telling you to Just Do It, I have a message for you.

No matter how many practical books your read, tips and tricks, writing hacks or videos you watch on crafting an epic story, if you can't put in the hard work and sit down to the dirty work, you will never be able to finish that book.

I'm not trying to be arrogant and I swear to god I'm trying just trying to drive my message home. I want you to nail it every single day. I want you to write even when you think you can't because you always can!

How bad do you want it?

That's for you to decide. Not for me. Not for anyone else. Just you.

If you want it bad enough, you've got to put in every bit of hard work that comes with the territory of writing.

Write Freely To Unleash The Beast

When I started writing my first fiction novel, I had my sights set on getting my manuscript published by a traditional publishing house. For some reason, there's a novelty attached to it. You've made it if a publishing house accepts your manuscripts and prints it for stores.

At the back of your mind, perhaps you too want this desire to be fulfilled.

That's perfectly okay.

It's a good goal to have.

However, if you're trying to improve your word count and actually finish a manuscript, the last thing you want to focus on is whether you're the best.

This may sound like counterintuitive advice.

And it is.

But, we live in a time when failure is at its highest.

People give up after the first attempt – especially if they feel as if it took everything they had to just finish a manuscript.

It's a damn shame.

Some of these writers could have produced amazing work if they hadn't given up.

I suggest abandoning your expectations. Allow time to play its course. Focus only on writing and let everything else manifest naturally.

Sure, this approach requires a strong sense of belief in yourself and the abandonment of control but if it guarantees you have a fighting chance at completing your book and having it submitted for acceptance, I consider that a win!

Most first drafts suck.

It's only after you write a completed draft are you capable of turning a mediocre draft into a superb one.

The editing and rewrite phase is when all the magic takes place. This is your time to apply makeup and Botox to your manuscript. Polish it up, cover and remove its flaws, highlight the best features and give it an overall good look.

So, write freely.

Don't worry yourself about grammar and typos. Only concern yourself with the story running like fluid and your fingers pacing through the keyboard as quickly as possible.

Write as if you are talking to someone extremely close to you. Think of it as telling a story to a person you love who is in desperate need of entertainment or education. What is the best approach at getting the message across?

What tone of voice and manner of speaking would make my dear loved one ball their eyes out in absolute enjoyment?

Use that question as a guideline and write freely.

You don't have to write like Shakespeare to sound artistic. You can try emulating famous authors, sure, but not if it means slowing down your own progress and growth.

What I do recommend is emulating the habits and writing patterns of an author who you identify with best. If you believe that your writing style is aligned with that of your favourite author, emulate his style.

It's not plagiarism to follow habits and structures of other writer's. Neither is similarity between ideas considered plagiarism as long as you had no intention to rip off someone else's work.

Using The Outer World To Create Your Inner World

When you write, you recreate.

Yes.

What you're doing is recreating the imagery and story in your mind. Writing is the means of transferring thoughts from your brain to the reader's brain.

But, where do you find a source of ideas and imagery in the first place?

Not everything is concocted inside your head.

On the contrary, everything around you is a source of ideas and content.

The air your breathe, the food you eat, the sounds you hear, the weather, the scenery, the sharp objects you feel and the overall emotions triggered by color. All of these elements feed your brain literary food.

Don't look but not see. Don't hear but not listen. Don't touch but not feel.

Engage your sense. Be aware of everything around you and use it to craft ideas and stories.

Let your environment, feelings and experiences guide you in writing a story.

Last night, I ate the most mouth-watering, cheesiest, soft to the touch and perfectly Italian spiced pasta I've ever eaten in my life. It was so well cooked that each piece of pasta literally melted in my mouth. The aroma of fresh spices knocked me off my chair and the feeling of pure joy and pleasure sent shivers down my spine and palette. My stomach was the happiest of me.

It was the perfect pasta.

And, I'm sure it was a piece of text that made you picture and remember the taste of pasta. I did that to you. I controlled your thoughts by appealing to your senses. How? Well, I used my own senses to write.

I was conscious of all my senses whilst eating pasta and it gave me enough material to craft that proper piece of descriptive text.

You see, you can't write for people unless you become people.

Experience life the way your target audience does. Understand how they feel, react and respond with all their senses to different things. Let that be your personal guide. At the end of the day, you will be writing for you and for your readers.

I guarantee that your work will not suffer but benefit extraordinarily from this simple technique.

You want to write more words, correct?

And you want to be able to write as much words as necessary without hitting a stone wall?

Well, this is how you do it.

Be aware of everything and describe everything you see, touch, smell, feel, experience, endure and think about.

The End Is Night

Alas, all good things must come to an end.

It's time for you to grab your pen, put your pants on and get to writing.

I believe in you and I want you to believe in yourself.

Impossible will always be impossible until you try to do it. Only then are you capable of actually doing the impossible.

Set a goal of writing 20 thousand words in 4 days, gather all the information you can possible get your hands on across all mediums, read over everything, highlight the best of information, write down all the important topics one after the other, draw a mind map and finally start writing with the intention of meeting your goal.

As a test, take a break from everything and see if you're capable of writing 20000 words in 4 days.

Unplug from society if you must but try winning this challenge.

If at the end of day 4 you've hit anywhere between 15 – 20 thousand words, you're golden.

You would have proven to yourself that writing high numbers and finishing that manuscript is indeed possible.

Put the advice in this book to good use.

Give it a read every day if you must.

This is your journey as a writer.

Embark on this journey without any regrets or reservations. Give everything you have and the world will give back to you.

I wish you luck.

Feel free to leave a review of this Book and subscribe to my mailing list for more. If anything, send me an email to let me know whether you were able to level up your word count! I'll keep an eye out for your email.

Until we meet again in another book.

Sincerely,

Zak.